SOLIDARITY WITH THE POOR

Sharing the Tradition
Shaping the Future Series

Book 5

Catholic Campaign for Human Development

United States Conference of Catholic Bishops • Washington, D.C.

In its formal 1995 planning document, as approved by the general membership of the National Conference of Catholic Bishops, the Catholic Campaign for Human Development was authorized "to develop relevant materials on social justice issues in order to raise the consciousness of parishioners. . . ." This present document was prepared under that authorization. The specific text was approved by the Executive Director of CCHD, Rev. Joseph R. Hacala, SJ, and was authorized for publication by the undersigned.

—Monsignor Dennis M. Schnurr
General Secretary, NCCB/USCC

In 2001 the National Conference of Catholic Bishops and United States Catholic Conference became the United States Conference of Catholic Bishops.

This booklet was prepared for the Catholic Campaign for Human Development by Christine A. W. Doby.

Scripture quotations, unless noted, are taken from the *New American Bible with Revised New Testament*. Copyright © 1986 by the Confraternity of Christian Doctrine, Washington, D.C., and are used with permission. All rights reserved.

ISBN 1-57455-192-2

First Printing, 1996
Third Printing, May 2003

CONTENTS

P oor and vulnerable people have a special place in Catholic social teaching. A basic moral test of a society is how its most vulnerable members are faring. This is not a new insight; it is the lesson of the parable of the Last Judgment (see Matthew 25:31-46). Our tradition calls us to put the needs of the poor and vulnerable first. As Christians, we are called to respond to the needs of all our sisters and brothers, but those with the greatest needs require the greatest response. We must seek creative ways to expand the emphasis of our nation's founders on individual rights and freedom by extending democratic ideals to economic life and thus ensure that the basic requirements for life with dignity are accessible to all" (*A Century of Social Teaching: A Common Heritage, a Continuing Challenge*, pp. 6-7).

The material in this booklet was prepared to offer members of the faith-sharing group an opportunity to explore Catholic social teaching on the subject of solidarity with the poor. In each of the six-week sessions, various subthemes of the major theme are treated, such as the meaning of solidarity, the human family and solidarity, the responsibility of solidarity, the work of solidarity, and the fruit of solidarity.

The meetings begin with a reflection (with the exception of the first week) on the prior week's discussion and actions. The reflection is followed by a Scripture reading by one of the group's members. All are invited to a silent reflection on the Scripture passage. You will note many other Scripture and church document references scattered throughout the reflections. These are to assist the group in filling in the rich tradition of church teachings. It is highly advisable for each member to read over each week's material before coming together as a group. This will allow members to follow up on the references they find most engaging and bring them to the whole group. Advance preparation will strengthen the group's reading of the material together and allow more time for prayer and reflection.

Focus questions are offered to help stimulate discussion and exploration of the subtheme and its implications. Participants' reliance on the power and grace of the Holy Spirit may provide for a lively discussion leading to greater openness to God's message about social justice.

Below are suggested opening and closing prayers. Any other form of prayer that a group prefers may be used.

To begin a group sharing experience, the following prayer may be used:
> Lord our God, we bless you.
> As we come together to ponder the Scriptures,
> we ask you in your kindness
> to fill us with the knowledge of your will
> so that, pleasing you in all things,
> we may grow in every good work.
> We ask this through Christ our Lord. Amen.

At the end of each session, the following prayer may be used:
> May God, the source of all patience and encouragement,
> enable us to live in perfect harmony with one another
> in the spirit of Christ Jesus.
> With one heart and one voice
> may we glorify God, now and forever. Amen.*

SUGGESTED ACTIONS

The format offered here is only a suggestion. Individual communities should feel free to alter their experience in whatever way appropriate. For instance, a group may wish to focus on one action taken together throughout the six weeks rather than on individual actions done each week. Whatever the format, it is strongly suggested that over the six-week period, some effort be made by the participants or the group to visit a low-income community. Participants would choose a site nearest work, parish, or home and visit the neighborhood two or three times over the six weekly meetings. They are encouraged to get a sense of the activities, sights and sounds, businesses, schools, recreational opportunities, and the people of the area. This will ground their action discussions and enrich their prayer and reflections as the group becomes a community of faith.

The Catholic Campaign for Human Development is an education/action program of the U.S. Catholic bishops to help bring about social justice. With the support of Catholic parishioners, the Catholic Campaign for Human Development carries out this mission in two ways: first, by funding and supporting self-help groups whose membership is primarily made up of economically disadvantaged people who organize to improve conditions that affect their lives, and second, by educating U.S. Catholics on the issues of social justice, especially as those issues relate to low-income people. At the heart of both of these efforts is the hope

---

*The opening and closing prayers are taken from *Catholic Household Blessings and Prayers*, available from the USCC, 3211 Fourth Street, NE, Washington, DC 20017-1194, or call 800-235-USCC (8722).

of empowering people to fully participate and enjoy the freedom, rights, and responsibilities that our communities, our nation, and indeed the world, have to offer.

Church documents used in this series are referenced by the following abbreviations:

GS   *Gaudium et Spes* (Vatican II, 1965)

SR   *Sollicitudo Rei Socialis* (Pope John Paul II, 1987)

ST   *Century of Social Teaching* (USCC, 1990)

Texts of these and other church documents are available from the USCC Office for Publishing and Promotion Services at 800-235-8722. The Catholic Campaign for Human Development has produced a 37-page booklet on the major themes of Catholic social teaching, *Principles, Prophecy and a Pastoral Response*, available directly from the Campaign at 800-946-4CHD.

THEME FOR THE WEEK
The Meaning of Solidarity

OPENING PRAYER

SCRIPTURE READING
John 17:21-23
> "So that they may all be one, as you, Father, are in me and
> I in you, that they also may be in us, that the world may
> believe that you sent me. And I have given them the glory
> you gave me, so that they may be one, as we are one, I in
> them and you in me, that they may be brought to perfec-
> tion as one, that the world may know that you sent me,
> and that you loved them even as you loved me."

SILENT REFLECTION BY THE GROUP

REFLECTION
What does the word "solidarity" evoke? The American union movement
of the '30s and '40s? The Polish freedom movement of the '80s? Other
ideas? No ideas? Does it evoke an image of the Church?

In fact, solidarity is well-rooted in the Catholic Church—literally,
well-rooted. The root word of solidarity is the Latin word, "sol," meaning
"whole." The Greek translation is "holo," as in cat<u>holic</u>—whole, universal.
There is a rooted connection between the word that describes our
Church and this word we are now exploring.

The dictionary defines solidarity as "a union of purposes or sympathies;
fellowship of responsibilities and interests; an intensification of unity."
Look again at Jesus' prayer cited above. Was he not praying for solidarity?

With whom did Jesus experience solidarity? With the disciples, surely: "I
have called you friends, because I have told you everything I have heard
from my Father" (John 15:15); and with all believers: "Whoever does
the will of my heavenly Father is my brother, and sister, and mother"
(Matthew 12:50). Indeed, we believe that Jesus experiences solidarity
with us, and we with him: "The cup of blessing that we bless, is it not a
participation in the blood of Christ? The bread that we break, is it not a
participation in the body of Christ?" (1 Corinthians 10:16).

Jesus also experienced solidarity with the despised of society: tax collectors (Mark 2:16), a woman well known in her town as a sinner (Luke 7:38-39), and others who were on the margins of the community's life. The ministry of Jesus gives witness to an important aspect of solidarity from a Christian perspective: There is no person, group, nation, nationality, class, race, religion, or human concern that is outside the loving care of God—and therefore, of God's Church. This is why the Church has said of itself, "The joys and hopes, the griefs and the anxieties of the [people] of this age, especially those who are poor or in any way afflicted, these are the joys and hopes, the griefs and the anxieties of the followers of Christ" (GS, 1).

We are, indeed, "one human family, whatever our national, racial, ethnic, economic, and ideological differences" (ST, p. 7). The word *solidarity* expresses our recognition of the unity of the human family. Christians do share the "joys and hopes, the griefs and anxieties . . . especially [of] those who are poor or in any way afflicted" (GS, 1). This is *not* "a feeling of vague compassion or shallow distress" at the misfortunes of others, but rather "a firm and persevering determination to commit oneself to the common good" (SR, 38). John Paul II has said that solidarity is "undoubtedly a Christian virtue" (SR, 40). This virtue "helps us to see the 'other'—whether a person, people or nation . . . as our 'neighbor,' a 'helper,' to be made a sharer, on a par with ourselves, in the banquet of life" (SR, 39).

Cultivating the virtue of solidarity helps us to live out Jesus' prayer that our unity may be complete so that the world will know the truth of the Gospel.

FOCUS QUESTIONS FOR GROUP DISCUSSION

1. How would you express the meaning of solidarity in your own words? What examples of solidarity can you share?

2. Compare Jesus' prayer for unity with the dictionary definition of solidarity and the quote from *Gaudium et Spes* (see above). Do you find commonalities?

3. Can you recall times when have you/your family/your parish gave witness to solidarity with "those who are poor or in any way afflicted"? Can you recall failures to offer such witness? What makes this difficult?

4. What are some of the barriers to human solidarity? Where do they come from?

SUGGESTED ACTIONS

1. Make a list of the joys, hopes, griefs, and anxieties
   - In your personal life
   - In your community
   - In the lives of those who are poor or afflicted

   Reflect this week on the similarities.

2. While watching TV or reading the newspaper this week, note any "them" and "us" bias (divisive reporting or stereotyping) in covering crimes or politics. Be prepared to share your observations next session.

CLOSING PRAYER

THEME FOR THE WEEK
The Human Family and Solidarity

OPENING PRAYER

GROUP REFLECTION
Group reflection on last week's session and actions

SCRIPTURE READING
Ephesians 2:13
> But now in Christ Jesus you who once were far off have
> become near by the blood of Christ.

SILENT REFLECTION BY THE GROUP

REFLECTION
Are we really one human family? For the moment, put aside questions of
how we treat each other. Just ask yourself if you truly believe that we
are one human family. Is the drug addict in Los Angeles your sister? Is
the farmer in Kansas your uncle? Is the AIDS baby in Detroit your child?
Is the stockbroker in New York your brother? Is the widow in San
Antonio your mother?

It is one thing to give intellectual assent to the notion that we are all
members of one human family. It is quite another to *believe* that we are
family. Cultivating the virtue of solidarity helps us to grow in our belief
that we are one family, with God as Father and Mother to us all.

This is a demanding Christian discipline. Our own intimate families are
often challenging enough. Add to that our immediate neighbors or co-
workers, and we have about as much "family" as many of us can handle.

Yet it is Christ's will for us to experience ourselves as one human family.
We have "one Lord, one faith, one baptism; one God and Father of all,
who is over all and through all and in all" (Ephesians 4:5-6). And if,
indeed, God is Father of us all and Jesus is brother of us all, then clearly
our Christian family love is meant to extend to all. Indeed, this is precisely
how the world will recognize the followers of Jesus: "This is how all
will know that you are my disciples, if you have love for one another"
(John 13:35).

It would be easier to develop the virtue of solidarity if only people were more lovable, if they would make better choices and decisions, if they would try harder, or if they were less demanding and more grateful. Recognizing this, Jesus issued this challenge: "For if you love those who love you, what credit is that to you? . . . And if you do good to those who do good to you, what credit is that to you? . . . If you lend money to those from whom you expect repayment, what credit [is] that to you? Even sinners lend to sinners. . . . Be merciful. . . . Stop judging. . . . Stop condemning. . . . Forgive. . . . Give . . ." (Luke 6:32-38).

It would also be easier to develop the virtue of solidarity if we didn't so often feel that we are on the "giving end" of Jesus' teachings—" 'Whatever you did for one of these least brothers [and sisters] of mine, you did for me. . . . What you did not do for one of these least ones, you did not do for me'" (Matthew 25:40, 45). But the reality is that *we are always on the receiving end*: "For God so loved the world that he gave his only Son, so that everyone who believes in him might not perish but might have eternal life" (John 3:16). There is no amount of doing "for the least of these" that can match what we have been freely given, for by God's "great mercy we have been born anew to a living hope through the resurrection of Jesus Christ from the dead" (1 Peter 1:3, NIV).

In Christ, we have all been made into one human family: "[You] were at that time without Christ, alienated from the community of Israel and strangers to the covenants of promise, without hope and without God in the world. But now in Christ Jesus you who once were far off have become near by the blood of Christ" (Ephesians 2:12-13).

Cultivating the virtue of solidarity helps us to believe that we are one human family: God has created us that way, and Jesus has strengthened those bonds with his blood.

FOCUS QUESTIONS FOR GROUP DISCUSSION

1. Allow group members to share an instance of a "them" vs. "us" bias in the media during the past week and to say what feelings it evoked.

2. This week's reflection asserts that it is God's will that we see ourselves as members of one human family. Do you think this is true? Explain.

3. This week's reflection suggests that it is easier to give intellectual assent to the concept that we are one human family than to *believe* in our hearts that we are one human family. Do you agree or disagree? Explain.

4. What are some of the barriers that keep us from seeing ourselves as one human family? Where do they come from? How do they work?

SUGGESTED ACTIONS

1. Clip a photo of someone you do not know, and may not typically associate with, from a newspaper, magazine, or other source. Keep the photo in an accessible place (near your bed, on your desk) and practice the virtue of solidarity with that one person—think of him or her as your brother or sister, imagine his or her hopes and fears, extend your heart in love and prayer for this person.

2. Investigate organizations that serve the stranger, refugee, migrant laborer, new immigrant, or low-income communities in your area. To help you practice solidarity, consider giving time or money to their cause.

CLOSING PRAYER

THEME FOR THE WEEK
The Responsibility of Solidarity

OPENING PRAYER

GROUP REFLECTION
Group reflection on last week's session and actions

SCRIPTURE READING
Genesis 4:9
> "Am I my brother's keeper?"

SILENT REFLECTION BY THE GROUP

REFLECTION
If in solidarity we develop the capacity to see all other persons as our brothers and sisters, does it follow that we have any responsibility to them? This is a question that is at least as old as Scripture.

The author of Genesis is a person awestruck by the wonder of the world. Inspired by faith that God is the author of all that exists, the writer recounts the story of creation, with the high point of God's creative energy being the creation of the human family.

But almost as soon as the story of humanity begins, trouble occurs. Adam and Eve are disobedient to God and are cast out of the Garden. Then, just a few verses later, Cain attacks his brother Abel and kills him. Barely into the fourth chapter of the Bible, the responsibility of solidarity is questioned: "Am I my brother's keeper?"

The responsibility of solidarity is raised again and again in Scripture. Certainly Moses was faced with this question. After all, in Egypt he didn't live in slavery—it wasn't his problem. He had plenty of problems of his own. Was he supposed to be his brothers' and sisters' keeper? In the end, Moses went to Pharaoh because he said yes to the question. The prophets, too, faced this question. They had their own lives to live, their own business to attend to. Yet they shared God's messages with people they didn't even know because they said yes to the question.

The responsibility of solidarity has also been raised by the Church as it seeks to serve the world: "The Church seeks but a solitary goal: to carry forward the work of Christ . . . under the lead of the befriending Spirit. And Christ entered this world to give witness to the truth, to rescue and not to sit in judgment, to serve and not to be served" (GS, 3). Through many institutions and structures, the Church seeks to carry forward the work of Christ through service.

The responsibility of solidarity also confronts every Christian. Solidarity requires a discipline of love. This does not refer to the emotion or feeling of love. Rather, this refers to a conscious act of the will—the choice to behave lovingly, regardless of our feelings: "Let mutual love continue. Do not neglect hospitality, for through it some have unknowingly entertained angels. Be mindful of prisoners as if sharing their imprisonment, and of the ill-treated as of yourselves, for you also are in the body" (Hebrews 13:1-3).

For Christians, the definitive answer regarding the responsibility of solidarity was given by Jesus when he answered the question "And who is my neighbor?" (Luke 10:29). According to Jesus, the Law of God could be summarized this way: Love God with all your heart, soul, strength, and mind, and love your neighbor as yourself (see Luke 10:27-28). Telling the parable of the good Samaritan, Jesus taught that the person who acts in solidarity with another, someone who is not known nor perhaps even liked, is the one who behaves as "neighbor." Jesus' instruction to us is "Go and do likewise" (Luke 10:37), for the followers of Jesus are their brothers' and sisters' keepers.

FOCUS QUESTIONS FOR GROUP DISCUSSION

1. If you haven't done so yet, allow members of the group to share any experiences of solidarity during the past week, especially as they may relate to last week's suggested activity.

2. Can you think of examples of people in the news who have responded to the responsibility of solidarity?

3. Do you know of activities of your parish, diocese, or the larger U.S. Catholic Church to serve those in need?

4. What actions might people undertake to develop a discipline of love?

5. What are some of the social barriers to responding yes to the question, "Am I my brother's or sister's keeper?"

SUGGESTED ACTIONS

1. Gather more information on one or more of the following:
   - Catholic Campaign for Human Development (800-946-4CHD)
   - Catholic Relief Services (800-736-3467)
   - Catholic Migration and Refugee Services (202-541-3352)
   - Diocesan Catholic social services (check with local diocese)

   How can you and/or your parish participate in these works?

2. Practice the discipline of love by finding a way to "entertain strangers" with a few words of conversation or hospitality, either at home with family members you don't see often, at work, on the street, through your parish, or in your community.

CLOSING PRAYER

THEME FOR THE WEEK
The Work of Solidarity

OPENING PRAYER

GROUP REFLECTION
Group reflection on last week's session and actions

SCRIPTURE READING
1 John 3:18
> Let us love not in word or speech but in deed and truth.

SILENT REFLECTION BY THE GROUP

REFLECTION
These sessions have asserted that solidarity is rooted in the Church. The virtue of solidarity helps us to see that all persons are members of one family under God and strengthens us to act responsibly in that relationship. The work of solidarity is love in action: "Let us love not in word or speech but in deed and truth" (1 John 3:18).

There may be no subject in Scripture so fully addressed as the work of solidarity. The Psalms praise God, who loves justice and mercy and hears the cries of the poor; the Proverbs remind us to listen to and be kind to the poor. The prophets cry out for justice (for example: Isaiah 5:7-16; Jeremiah 22:13-16; Ezekiel 16:49; Amos 4:1-3, 5:12-15, 23-24, and 8:4-7). Solidarity is eloquently summarized by Micah: "[Do] what the LORD requires of you: / Only to do the right and to love goodness, / and to walk humbly with your God" (6:8).

Mary praises God who "has thrown down the rulers from their thrones / but lifted up the lowly. / The hungry he has filled with good things; / the rich he has sent away empty" (Luke 1:52-53). It is no wonder that her son, Jesus, begins his public ministry with the proclamation

> The Spirit of the Lord is upon me,
> because he has anointed me
> to bring glad tidings to the poor.
> He has sent me to proclaim liberty to captives
> and recovery of sight to the blind,

to let the oppressed go free,
and to proclaim a year acceptable to the Lord. (Luke 4:18-19)

One can hardly open the Scriptures without finding reference to God's command to live our lives in solidarity, especially with those who are poor. There are two primary aspects to the work of solidarity: direct service and social justice.

Direct service involves the works of charity. St. James writes, "If a brother or sister has nothing to wear and has no food for the day, and one of you says to them, 'Go in peace, keep warm, and eat well,' but you do not give them the necessities of the body, what good is it? So also faith of itself, if it does not have works, is dead" (2:15-17). Christian faith in "charitable" action has led to the founding of soup kitchens, shelters, hospitals, counseling agencies, child care programs, and countless other direct services that respond to immediate human needs. The Church teaches, however, that what is due in justice cannot be offered as a gift of charity and so the demands of justice must first be met before true charity can be exercised (see *Catechism of the Catholic Church*, no. 2446).

Social justice, then, is work that seeks to change the conditions in society which contribute to poverty or oppression. Social justice makes true charity possible by meeting the demands of justice: "Learn to do good. / Make justice your aim: redress the wronged, / hear the orphan's plea, defend the widow" (Isaiah 1:17); "the loot wrested from the poor is in your houses. / What do you mean by crushing my people, / and grinding down the poor when they look to you?" (Isaiah 3:14-15). The work for social justice is accomplished by working in the community for changes in laws, policies, programs, and social or economic institutions for the reallocation of resources.

Our church communities have been much better at the work of direct service than the work of social justice. For one thing, we have more experience with direct service. And it is usually quite clear what needs to be done: feed the hungry, shelter the homeless, visit the prisoner, etc. It must also be said that direct service is often borne out of an emergency response. Only later do we tend to realize deeper solutions are required.

On the other hand, social justice is frequently less straightforward and comes after careful reflection and planning. We may share the goal of providing housing, but where, when, and how to do so is less clear. And social justice is often controversial. While no one wants sick people to go without medical treatment, people disagree vehemently on the means of providing access and care.

Yet direct service may not always constitute the best use of our time and resources. Consider this story: One day a woman finds a baby floating by in a river. She rescues the child and adopts it. The next day, there are two babies in the river; one is dead. She provides for a burial and finds a family for the other baby. In succeeding days, more babies come down the river. Before long there are committees to care for the sick, provide homes for the healthy, and bury the dead. In time, the community's resources are stretched to their limits. Finally, it occurs to the woman to go upstream and find out how and why the babies are ending up in the river. This is the work of social justice: to go against the stream and address the source of the problem; to change the systems, structures, and conditions of society which are causing hurt. This is the work of solidarity.

Clearly God expects our charitable responses to encompass both service and justice:

> This, rather, is the fasting that I wish:
>> releasing those bound unjustly,
>> untying the thongs of the yoke;
> Setting free the oppressed,
>> breaking every yoke;
> Sharing your bread with the hungry,
>> sheltering the oppressed and the homeless;
> Clothing the naked when you see them. (Isaiah 58:6-7)

In fact, our solidarity with the poor is the sign of God's life in us: "If someone who has worldly means sees a brother [or sister] in need and refuses him [or her] compassion, how can the love of God remain in him [or her]?" (1 John 3:17).

The work of solidarity is also true worship of God:

> I take no pleasure in your solemnities;
> Your cereal offerings I will not accept,
>> nor consider your stall-fed peace offerings.
> Away with your noisy songs!
>> I will not listen to the melodies of your harps.
> But if you would offer me holocausts,
>> then let justice surge like water,
>> and goodness like an unfailing stream. (Amos 5:21-24)

FOCUS QUESTIONS FOR GROUP DISCUSSION

1. Discuss your understanding of the difference between direct service and social justice.

2. What are some ways parishes are involved in direct service work? In work for social justice?

3. What social justice issues might the Church address which would mitigate the need for a direct service response to poverty-related issues such as homelessness, hunger, and crime?

4. What are some of the social barriers that keep parishes from being actively involved in social justice concerns? What would you be willing to do to help your parish overcome them?

SUGGESTED ACTIONS

1. Check with your local diocese for information on Catholic legislative advocacy networks. Become active in a network.

2. Either on your own or with the help of the public library make a list of organizations in your community striving to improve the quality of justice. Contact the organizations to see how your parish might help promote and publicize their work.

3. Order the free *Resources for Justice Education and Action* catalog from the Catholic Campaign for Human Development, 800-946-4CHD. Work with your catechist coordinator or director of religious education to integrate these resources into their classes.

CLOSING PRAYER

THEME FOR THE WEEK
The Fruit of Solidarity

OPENING PRAYER

GROUP REFLECTION
Group reflection on last week's session and actions

SCRIPTURE READING
John 17:21-23; Luke 24:36

> "So that they may all be one, as you, Father, are in me and
> I in you, that they also may be in us, that the world may
> believe that you sent me. And I have given them the glory
> you gave me, so that they may be one, as we are one, I in
> them and you in me, that they may be brought to perfec-
> tion as one, that the world may know that you sent me,
> and that you loved them even as you loved me."
>
> While they were still speaking about this, he stood in their
> midst and said to them, "Peace be with you."

SILENT REFLECTION BY THE GROUP

REFLECTION
To reflect on the fruit of solidarity, we return to the same Scripture reading
we used during Session One, for one of the fruits of solidarity is the
same as its meaning: unity. The virtue of solidarity helps us understand
our relationship to all of God's people—we are one human family,
bound by the ties of God's creation and Christ's blood. The virtue of
solidarity helps us to answer the question "Am I my brother's or sister's
keeper?" by exploring the meaning of Jesus' teaching: "The first [com-
mandment] is this: '. . . You shall love the Lord your God with all your
heart, with all your soul, with all your mind, and with all your strength.'
The second is this: 'You shall love your neighbor as yourself.' There is
no other commandment greater than these" (Mark 12:29-31).

The exercise of solidarity through direct service unites Christians in our
common mission with Christ: "For the Son of Man did not come to be
served but to serve" (Mark 10:45). And although it is often demanding
and more challenging to do, the exercise of solidarity through the works

of social justice is also unitive—beyond the person-to-person level, to that of the systems which shape our economic and social worlds.

The work for social justice is about "us"—all of us. The purpose of social justice is to advance the common good. Adequate jobs at just wages are good for all of us; sufficient health care is good for all of us; decent, affordable housing is good for all of us; competent schools are good for all of us.

And social justice invites everyone into a role in the common good: "Those who are more influential . . . should feel responsible for the weaker and be ready to share with them all they possess. Those who are weaker, for their part, in the same spirit of solidarity, should not adopt a purely passive attitude or one that is destructive of the social fabric, but, while claiming their legitimate rights, should do what they can for the good of all. The intermediate groups, in their turn, should not selfishly insist on their particular interests, but respect the interests of others" (SR, 39).

Since the work of solidarity advances service, mercy, and justice, it follows that another fruit of solidarity will be peace: "Justice will bring about peace; / right will produce calm and security" (Isaiah 32:17). This wisdom is reflected in the motto of Pius XII, "Peace is the fruit of justice," and in one of the most famous sayings of Paul VI, "If you want peace, work for justice."

Preaching about solidarity, Pope John Paul II has said, "The solidarity which we propose is the path to peace. . . . For world peace is inconceivable unless the world's leaders come to recognize . . . interdependence" (SR, 39).

It must be admitted that there is frequently greater satisfaction in direct service: a family needs food, a teenager needs shelter, an elderly man needs medicine, and these needs are met. We all like immediate gratification. But we should resist the temptation to ignore the works of justice and peace because we do not see immediate effects, for these works bear good fruit for generations to come:

> Quasars, scientists teach, are ten trillion times more brilliant than ordinary stars such as the sun. They are so bright that they can be observed at distances more than 10 billion light years away from Earth. Some of the ones we see, in fact, have been dead for several billion years and their light is just reaching the Earth. When nothing you do seems to prosper, to take root, to grow, quasars teach us

not to despair. Some light comes later, long after it first dared to gleam. (Joan Chittister, as quoted in *Love Beyond Measure*, Pax Christi USA, 1993)

FOCUS QUESTIONS FOR GROUP DISCUSSION

1. How might the world be different today if unity and peace were predominant values?

2. Discuss the pros and cons of devoting your energies to social justice activities. Share what it would take for you to become involved in such an activity.

SUGGESTED ACTIONS

1. Obtain a copy of the *Catechism of the Catholic Church* or the Holy Father's most recent statement and work with the parish outreach team or pastor to start a study group on the featured social justice themes.

2. Contact Catholic Relief Services, 800-736-3467, and find out what it takes to adopt a project or parish in the developing world or sponsor its "Food Fast" or "Operation Rice Bowl" programs which build awareness of the developing world. Work with your parish council or pastor to make it happen.

3. Use the event of the Catholic Campaign for Human Development's collection in November, which celebrates the Church's solidarity with the poor, to build relations between a Catholic Campaign for Human Development-funded group and your parish. Contact your diocesan chancery for details, or call the national Catholic Campaign for Human Development office, 800-946-4CHD.

CLOSING PRAYER

(Note: The implementation of this week's activity can occur in Week Four, Five, or Six.)

THEME FOR THE WEEK
CCHD: Catholic Social Teaching in Action

OPENING PRAYER

REFLECTION
As called for by the Second Vatican Council, the Catholic bishops of the United States gathered together in 1969, to "read the signs of the times" and "apply the gospel message" to that examination. One very troubling sign the bishops identified was pervasive and unrelenting poverty in their communities. The bishops recognized that the Catholic Church had a long, proud history of addressing the painful *effects* of poverty through its numerous voluntary associations. However, there had never been an institutional response aimed at eliminating the *causes* of poverty, especially in a way that empowered low-income persons and their neighborhoods. Therefore, a vision to fund organized groups of low-income people who would identify their own problems and create solutions to those problems began to take shape. This process of empowerment was viewed as a genuine application of the gospel call to love our neighbor. Empowerment not only had the potential to create practical solutions to poverty issues, but it would do so in a way that preserved and enhanced the dignity of the human person.

From the start, the bishops also recognized that there was no possible way to collect and distribute enough money to eradicate poverty. What also had to be present was an effort to engage non-poor Catholics in a way that would move them to act in solidarity with organized poor people. The prescribed method was education that leads to conversion, which, in turn, leads to support for empowerment activities of the low-income community. The resulting partnership between the poor and non-poor would not only provide greater possibilities for actually solving problems of poverty, but also would be a vehicle for helping the non-poor truly understand specific themes of Catholic social teaching (i.e., "preferential option for/with the poor," "empowerment/life and dignity of the human person," and "the call to participation").

The dual focus of **empowerment** and **transformative education** became the mission of the Catholic Campaign for Human Development, which was officially established in 1970. Eighteen years later, in November 1988, the United States Catholic bishops enthusiastically recommitted themselves to this vision. In doing so, the Catholic Campaign for Human Development became a permanent program within the United States Catholic Conference.

To make sure empowerment and participation became more than simple rhetoric, the Campaign established a strict set of criteria and guidelines. All CCHD-funded projects must

- Set up a decision-making board of directors. Fifty percent of the board's membership must be low-income persons
- Generate cooperation among diverse groups of people
- Work to change conditions that create and/or perpetuate poverty
- Directly benefit a large number of people
- Develop plans for self-sufficiency

CCHD education, similarly, attempts to be practical, down-to-earth, and useful. The guiding principles for all CCHD education are to

- Be parish-based and develop faith through prayer and reflection on Scripture
- Provide organized opportunities to bring non-poor parishioners and organized poor people together so that each group can learn from the other
- Require activities to be well thought-out and planned
- Remember that conversion takes place over time and through action, not just words

Every time an organizing grant is made, an economic development project is approved, or an education activity is carried out, the Catholic Church as a faith community can stand proud. These actions reaffirm the words of Pope John Paul II: "This Campaign has been a witness to the church's living presence in the world among the most needy, and to her commitment to continuing the mission of Christ" (Chicago, Illinois, Providence of God Church: October 5, 1979).

SUGGESTED ACTIONS

1. Share the high points of your time together around a celebrational meal. Then decide if you will continue to meet as a faith group or start other groups in the parish to reflect on working for and with the poor. Consider using other booklets in this series.

2. Discuss your visits to the low-income communities mentioned at the beginning of this booklet. Then review the action suggestions from previous weeks. What would the group like to tackle?

3. Obtain from your diocesan director for the Catholic Campaign for Human Development a list of funded groups in your diocese or state. Discuss how these groups might be a resource to your parish and how to promote/publicize the issues of CCHD-funded groups in your area.

CLOSING PRAYER

NOTES

NOTES